NIMIT RATHOD

Market Mavericks

Young Investor's Guide to Basics of Stock Market

In loving memory of my ideal, the Late Mr. Harshad Mehta, whose passion for the stock market ignited my own curiosity and inspired me to delve deeper into the world of finance. Your wisdom, love, and inspiration continue to resonate within these pages.

"The stock market is filled with indi viduals who know the price of every thing, but the value of nothing." —Philip Fisher

Contents

Foreword

As a high school student with a fascination for the intricacies of the stock market and the financial world, I embarked on a journey to unravel its mysteries and share my learning with fellow young enthusiasts. In this book, I present a beginner friendly guide to the stock market, designed specifically for young readers eager to explore the exciting world of finance. Throughout my own exploration of the stock market, I've encountered numerous challenges and uncertainties. However, I've also discovered a wealth of knowledge and opportunities waiting to be tapped. With this book, I aim to demystify the complexities of investing and provide a solid foundation for young readers to begin their own financial journey. From understanding basic concepts such as stocks and index to exploring more advanced topics like risk management, this book covers a wide range of essential principles in a clear and accessible manner. Through this book, readers will learn how to make informed investment decisions and navigate the ups and downs of the market with confidence. While the stock market may seem daunting at first, I believe that with the right guidance and mindset, anyone can become a successful investor.I hope this book inspires you to embark on your own journey of financial exploration and empowers you to take control of your financial future. Happyreading, and may your adventures in the stock market iii be both enlightening and rewarding!

Preface

Dear Readers, In today's fast-paced world, the stock market plays a pivotal role in shaping our economy and influencing our lives. It is my firm belief that understanding the basics of the stock market is not only essential but also empowering. This book is born out of a simple yet profound conviction: that knowledge is the key to unlocking the doors of opportunity. Whether you're a student, a young professional, or simply curious about the world of finance, mastering the basics of the stock market is a crucial first step towards building a solid foundation for your financial journey.

Acknowledgement

I would like to express my heartfelt gratitude to my parents, Mr. Nilesh Rathod and Mrs. Ranjeeta Rathod, whose unwavering support, encouragement, and belief in me have been the driving force behind the creation of this book. Their boundless love, guidance, and motivation have been my constant inspiration throughout this journey. I am truly blessed to have them by myside, and I dedicate this book to them with all my love and appreciation. Their encouragement has fueled my passion for writing and their unwavering faith in my abilities has been the cornerstone of my success. Thank you, Mom and Dad, for always believing in me.

A Beginner's Guide to the Stock Market!

Hi there, ambitious financial wizard! We're heading on an amazing adventure into the stock market world today. If you've never heard of it before, don't worry; we'll start from the beginning and make it very simple to understand. So grab a seat, and let's explore the exciting world of stocks!

Definition of the Stock Market

Imagine you want to create the greatest lemonade stand in the neighborhood for your lemonade sale. To do that, though, you'll need cash to buy more cups, sugar, and lemons. This is where the stock market enters the picture. It represents a large marketplace where individuals may purchase and sell little portions of businesses, just like your lemonade stand.

In grown-up terms, these tiny parts are"stocks." A stock represents a small portion of a company's ownership. In other words, if your lemonade stand was a business and you sold stocks to the public, other individuals may purchase those stocks and take a stake in your lemonade stand. Nice, huh!

How Is It Operated?

Let's now discuss how the stock market operates. Businesses sell their stock to individuals such as your parents or to other businesses. Prices increase when a company's stock attracts a large number of buyers. When consumer interest decreases the price may decrease. It's similar to when the price of the newest video game increases because everyone wants to buy it.

Owners of stocks have two ways to profit. First, the value of the company's stocks may increase if it performs well and sells a lot of lemonade (or whatever it sells). It's similar to when your lemonade stand gains enormous popularity and everyone wants to be a part of it.

Conclusion

So, there you have it, our little adventure into the stock market! It's like a big game where you can be part of amazing companies and watch your money grow. Just remember to be patient, do some research on the companies you want to invest in, and have fun learning about this cool world of stocks. Who knows, maybe one day you'll be the owner of the next big thing, just like your very own lemonade stand!

Investing vs. Trading: Which Is Right for You?

I ndividuals frequently have to choose between trading and investing in order to increase their wealth in the world of financial markets. There are two ways to get involved in the financial markets: trading and investing. However, the two have quite different approaches, timing, and risk tolerance. The differences between trading and investing are examined in the following paragraphs, along with the important variables that students should take into account while choosing the course that best suits their financial objectives.

The Time Machine Ride:Investing

See the investment track as a methodical, gradual time machine. Investors board, fasten their seatbelts, and get ready for a comfortable ride into the future. The objective stays the same: observe your wealth increase over time, despite changes in the environment and economics. It's similar like planting a money tree and seeing it grow.

Example: You invest in a tech company's stock because you think its future advancements will be revolutionary. Instead of constantly monitoring the stock market, you're happy to ride along with the knowledge that your investment will increase in value over time.

2. The Ultimate Twister: Exchange

Let's now shift gears to the trade track, where quick reflexes, agility, and heart-pounding thrills are key components. Like Formula 1 drivers, traders must make split-second judgments while handling hairpin curves and straightaways. It's a thrilling ride with rapid gains (or losses).

Example: You choose to make a profit on a trend in bitcoin prices by buying into it. Catching waves, making short deals, and expecting to ride out with a pocket full of gains before the next big wave is your game plan. You are not in it for the long run.

3. The Dangerous Rapids: The White Water Journey of Trading

Trading in the financial river is similar to white-water rafting. Although the rapids are thrilling, there is a genuine chance of being wet or saturated. In order to get that big gain, traders embrace volatility, navigate through market swings, and occasionally even take a risky dive over a waterfall.

For instance, you are trading options on a popular stock. Prices are rising and falling, making it a fast ride. You're maneuvering through the turns and curves, planning every step to get through the rapids and emerge with a profit.

4. The Castle of Compound Returns: The Grand Finale of Investing

The massive Castle of Compound Returns is reached via the investing pathway. The longer you remain, the more impressive the castle gets, but it's not an overnight vision. The compound magic, where money makes money and the castle gets more and more magnificent over time, is what investors enjoy.

As an illustration, let's say you regularly allocate a percentage of your income to a diversified portfolio. Your castle expands with time as interest and profits add to the grand design. It's about the timeless beauty of compound growth, not dazzling explosions.

Conclusion

Trading and investing provide different rollercoaster sensations in this financial amusement park. Investing is like taking a beautiful, long-term trip that could conclude with a magnificent compound castle. The thrilling adventure of trading is full of turns, twists, and the occasional white-water surge. Thus, choose the path that best fits your style and enjoy the incredible journey to financial success, whether you're in it for the steady ascent or the adrenaline rush!

Understanding the Practical Process of Buying and Selling Stocks

Introduction

The global economy depends heavily on stock markets, which give investors a platform to purchase and sell ownership holdings in businesses. Purchasing and selling stocks is a fundamental part of the financial markets, despite its initial complexity. We will look at the actual procedures associated with purchasing and selling stocks in this chapter, simplifying the technical terms and offering a clear explanation of this crucial financial action.

1. Setting the Stage: Understanding Stocks and Stock Markets

It's important to understand the fundamentals before diving into the purchasing and selling process. Shares of ownership in a firm are represented by stocks, which are bought and sold on the stock market. In order to raise money, businesses issue stocks, which investors purchase in the hope of making money from the company's expansion.

2. Selecting a Platform: Conventional Brokerage Firms against Online Brokerages

Investors have several options when it comes to purchasing and selling stocks in the current digital era. The popularity of online brokerage platforms has increased due to their less fees and easy-to-use interfaces. Though they are less common, traditional brokerage firms offer personalized support and guidance. Investors can select a platform according to their requirements and preferences.

3. Creating an Account: The First Step to Trading

To participate in the stock market, individuals need to open a brokerage account. This involves providing personal information, funding the account, and agreeing to the terms and conditions. Online platforms often streamline this process, allowing users to create accounts quickly.

4. Investing in Stocks: Making Well-Informed Decisions

It is important to investigate the stocks of interest before making any kind of investment. Investors need to assess a company's performance, economic situation, and possibilities for growth.Online platforms provide access to financial reports, analyst recommendations, and historical stock prices to aid in informed decision-making.

5. Placing an Order: Executing the Trade

An investor must submit an order to purchase or sell a stock after selecting it. Market orders and limit orders are the two main categories of orders. A limit order indicates a desired price, and the trade is performed only if the market hits it. In contrast, a market order directs the broker to execute the trade instantly at the current market price.

6. Transaction Confirmation: Ensuring Accuracy

Investors receive a transaction confirmation with all the trade details after placing an order. Reviewing this confirmation is essential to make sure all the details are right, such as the stock, amount, and pricing. Any variations must be brought up right away with the brokerage.

7. Investment Management and Monitoring: An Ongoing Process

Trading stocks successfully involves more than just the initial transaction. Investors should keep a close eye on their portfolios and stay up to date on company and market changes. Stop-loss orders, which automatically sell a stock if its price drops below a preset level, can be used to assist control risks.

In summary

To sum up, purchasing and selling stocks is an incredibly simple procedure that enables anybody to take part in the exciting world of finance. An investor can confidently explore the stock market by knowing the fundamentals, selecting the appropriate platform, carrying out extensive research, and placing well-informed trades. Investments are continuously managed and monitored to provide a proactive strategy for financial success. The fascinating and potentially lucrative world of stock trading is becoming more accessible to a wider audience due to technological advancements that make the process easier to understand.

Exploring Different Stock Exchanges!

Introduction

With a platform for share purchases and sales, stock exchanges are a vital component of the financial system. Here we will explore the world of stock exchanges, focusing especially on India's oldest and most well-known exchange, the Bombay Stock Exchange (BSE). We'll discover the unique features that characterize them apart as we navigate through a variety of exchanges and investigate their contributions to the global financial scene.

1. Bombay Stock Exchange (BSE)

Founded in 1875, the Bombay Stock Exchange is a historic establishment situated in Mumbai, India. As an indication of the state of the Indian economy, the BSE is a major participant in the financial market. It features a wide range of businesses from industries like manufacturing, technology, and finance. The BSE, which offers an opportunity for wealth generation and capital building, has been essential to India's economic success.

2. New York Stock Exchange (NYSE)

Located on Wall Street, the New York Stock Exchange is a well-known representation of international finance. It is well known for having a sizable trading floor and strict listing guidelines. The NYSE is a major participant in the global financial ecosystem and the home of numerous multinational firms. By contrasting the NYSE with the BSE, one can see how these exchanges differ from one another in terms of size, composition, and legal frameworks.

3. NASDAQ

Now let's move to the US, where the NASDAQ is a tech-focused exchange. The whole NASDAQ trading floor is computerized, in contrast to traditional trading floors. It is known for listing technology giants like Apple, Microsoft, and Amazon. The growth of stock exchanges from conventional open outcry methods to completely automated electronic platforms is demonstrated by comparing the NASDAQ with the BSE.

4. London Stock Exchange (LSE)

Transitioning to Europe, the London Stock Exchange holds a prominent position in the international financial sphere. With a varied listing of businesses and a rich history, the London Stock Exchange (LSE) reflects London's cosmopolitan nature. By contrasting the LSE and the BSE, one can see how various exchanges serve various economies by mirroring local economic frameworks and cultural influences.

5. Shanghai Stock Exchange (SSE)

With China's economic growth, the Shanghai Stock Exchange has become more well-known throughout Asia. Reflecting China's shifting economic landscape, the SSE is home to a mix of private and state-owned businesses. By comparing the SSE with the BSE, one can see how emerging markets in the global financial system face particular possibilities as well as limitations.

Conclusion

In summary, studying different stock exchanges—with particular focus on the Bombay Stock Exchange—reveals the rich diversity of the world's financial marketplaces. Every exchange adds something different to the global economic symphony, whether it is the dynamic NASDAQ, the tech-savvy NYSE, the historic BSE, the cosmopolitan LSE, or the developing SSE. Youngsters who want to work in finance need to understand the complexities of various transactions and how they represent the technological, cultural, and economic environments of the places in which they operate. Despite a constantly evolving financial nature, stock exchanges such as the BSE continue to play a crucial role in determining the economic status of countries and making an impact on the interdependent global economy.

IPOs: A Beginner's Guide to Investing in Initial Public Offerings

Introduction

IPOs, or initial public offerings, signal a thrilling stage in a business's development. Knowing about initial public offerings (IPOs) can be a vital first step for students wishing to advance their investment education. A private firm can become public by first offering its shares to the general public through an initial public offering (IPO). The purpose of this chapter is to simplify initial public offers (IPOs) and provide students an understanding of the advantages and disadvantages of investing in these offerings

Understanding IPOs

The grand opening of a business in the stock market is similar to an IPO. A corporation is privately held prior to an IPO, which means that a small number of people or investors possess its shares. A corporation that chooses to go public sells stocks to the general public, releasing a portion of the company's ownership. Following that, investors can purchase these shares on the stock market. Typically, an IPO raises money for a variety of uses, including debt repayment, corporate expansion, and research & development funding.

Opportunities for Investors

For investors, taking part in an IPO might offer special benefits. If the company does well on the stock market, early investors can see significant capital gains. Investing in early-stage companies may bring emotional rewards for owners, as they become co-owners of a potentially lucrative enterprise. Also, by increasing exposure to other markets and industries, initial public offerings (IPOs) can broaden an investor's portfolio.

Risks Involved

Students should understand the risks involved in investing in initial public offerings (IPOs), despite their attraction of the possibility for financial gain. Because they frequently have no track record, newly public companies are difficult to evaluate in terms of long-term performance. IPO stock prices are often volatile, and the underlying value of the firm may not always be reflected in the mood of the market. Furthermore, there's a chance of oversubscription, which happens when there's more demand than there are shares available. This could raise share prices in the first few trading days.

Study and Careful Consideration

Students should do extensive research and investigation before thinking about making an investment in an initial public offering (IPO). It is essential to understand the business strategy, financial condition, competitive environment, and growth potential of the organization. Gaining important insights can come from reading the prospectus, a document that contains comprehensive information on the initial public offering. Additionally, keeping up with industry advancements, market trends, and economic conditions can help students make wise investment choices.

How to Participate in an IPO

To take part in an IPO, you have to follow certain steps. In order to make orders for the necessary amount of shares during the IPO's subscription period, investors usually need to register a brokerage account. It's critical to abide by the instructions given by the brokerage platform and to be informed of any requirements for eligibility or limitations. Setting a budget and resisting the urge to invest more than they can bear to lose are other important considerations for investors.

Conclusion

For students who are interested in investing, understanding initial public offerings (IPOs) is a crucial component of financial literacy. IPOs have inherent dangers in addition to the great potential they present for financial gain and ownership in expanding businesses. Through detailed investigation, exercising careful research, and being aware of possible obstacles, students can more confidently approach the world of initial public offering (IPO) investing. As they say, "knowledge is power," and having knowledge may help you make wise and profitable financial decisions when it comes to initial public offerings (IPOs).

Blue Chips vs. Penny Stocks: Know the Difference

Choosing between chocolate and vanilla ice cream when it comes to investing can be compared to a dessert menu where each person has their preferred taste. When it comes to stocks, it's important to know the various kinds of stocks available rather than just choosing one that sounds good. Let's take a tour of the stock market today, focusing on the fascinating and adventurous worlds of penny stocks and blue chips.

Blue Chips - The Superstars of Stocks

Imagine if stocks were like a talent show, and Blue Chip stock was the most talented of the financial world. These stocks are held by big, reputable businesses that have been operating for a long time. Consider the Wall Street titans: Apple, Google, and Amazon.

Why do they refer to them as "Blue Chips" now? It's not because they have a blueberry flavor, though. This phrase was taken from the poker industry, where the most valued chips are blue ones. These businesses are renowned for their stability, consistent performance, and overall trust; they are comparable to the stock market's superheroes.

However, try not to get too fascinated! These stocks are not immune to market ups and downs. They are not immune to difficult days; Superman too has times of weakness. Nonetheless, they are less likely to disappear into financial darkness given their extensive resources and lengthy history.

Penny Stocks - The Daredevils of Investing

Now, imagine stocks as a roller coaster, with penny stocks representing the twists and loops that make your stomach turn over. Like the thrill-seekers of the stock market, penny stocks are sometimes associated with riskier, smaller companies. These stocks are more accessible to the common person because they are generally affordable.

Why do they go by the name "Penny Stocks"? Well, these stocks used to just cost a few pennies in the past. Even though they are more expensive now, the term stayed. Purchasing Penny Stocks is similar to purchasing a lottery ticket in that there is always a chance you won't win big.

Like a rodeo ride, penny stocks can be thrilling, but the hazards are higher. These businesses might have a less stable financial history, and their stock prices might fluctuate as much as a balloon at a party. There is a chance to make enormous profits, but there is also a chance to lose your money.

The Big Differences - Let's Play Spot the Distinctions!

Consider penny stocks and blue chips to be the yin and yang of the stock market. Like pancakes and waffles, or cats and dogs, they are distinct in a million ways. Here are a few key difference to help you in the game "Spot the Distinctions":

Size of Company: Penny Stocks often come from smaller, less established enterprises, whereas Blue Chips are associated with larger, more established companies.

Price Per Share: Blue Chips can be very expensive; a share may cost thousands or even more than that. Conversely, penny stocks are very affordable, frequently costing only a few hundreds or even less than that.

Amount of Risk:Blue Chips are the responsible adults in the room – steady, reliable, and less inclined to wild swings. The riskiest investment option, penny stocks have the potential for enormous profits but also a larger chance of losing money.

Attention to the Market: Blue Chips attract a lot of attention from analysts and investors, much like the popular kids everyone wants to hang out with. Penny Stocks operate more like the forgotten ones, going unnoticed until they accomplish a stunning performance.

Which Stock Flavor Is Ideal for You?

After exploring the fascinating worlds of penny stocks and blue chips, it's time to decide which stock flavor best suits your portfolio. Are you willing to take risks and are you excited about the potential for success with penny stocks? Or, while giving up the feeling of excitement, do you like Blue Chips' consistency and dependability.

Finding the ideal balance for you is crucial. Perhaps you'd prefer a little of both: a hint of roller coaster thrill mixed with a hint of Hollywood glamor. Your investments should withstand you from market fluctuations if you diversify them, much like a variety of different stocks.

Ultimately, keep in mind that investing is a trip, regardless of whether you're drinking Blue Chip tea or experiencing the Penny Stock roller coaster. It's about developing, learning, and sometimes finding amusement in the unique sense of humor that is the stock market. So fasten your seatbelt, grab your superman costume, and let the journey start!

Notable Stock Market Disasters and the Lessons They Teach Us

Introduction

The stock market has seen a variety of ups and downs throughout history, making it an exciting playground for investors. The lowest points can be frightening and even disastrous, while the highs provide happiness and wealth. We will explore the most well-known stock market crashes and the insightful lessons that can be drawn from them.

The 1929 Wall Street Crash and the Great Depression

The Great Depression, commonly referred to as the Wall Street Crash of 1929, remains to be a crucial moment in financial history. Excessive speculation, unsustainable debt, and economic imbalances caused the stock market to collapse, which erased fortunes over night.This crash has taught us the value of understanding market fundamentals, the necessity of limiting excessive risk, and the uncontrollable effects of speculating. Investors need to keep in mind that sustained growth is predicated on a strong basis and be careful of the attraction of rapid gains.

The Bubble in Dot-Coms Burst

Fast forward to the late 1990s, and the world witnessed the rise of the dot-com bubble.The promises of the emerging internet sector fascinated investors, who poured money into businesses that made little or no profit. Several investors watched as their portfolios were completely destroyed as the bubble burst in the early 2000s.The lesson here is the significance of due diligence.Even while emerging industries and technology could seem promising, overconfidence can have disastrous results. Investors must examine companies closely, paying attention to possible business plans as well as marketing hype.

The Financial Crisis of 2008

The global economy was devastated by the 2008 financial crisis, which was caused by the collapse of the housing market. A global recession resulted from the failure of financial institutions. We learned the value of risk management and the interdependence of financial markets from the disaster. Important lessons from this era include diversification, recognizing the possible effects of one industry on another, and exercising precaution when analyzing risks. Pupils need to understand that seemingly unconnected events can have a catastrophic effect on the financial system as a whole.

Black Monday – 1987

Black Monday, October 19, 1987, saw a 22% drop in the stock market. The primary causes of the disaster were identified as programmed selling and computerized trading, highlighting the importance of technology in the financial system. The lesson here is that technology improvements need to be regulated and closely observed. Technology has definitely changed the way we invest, but if it is not used appropriately, there are risks involved. It is essential that students realize the need of maintaining awareness regarding market systems and potential consequences of excessive technology advancement.

Conclusion

In conclusion, investors may learn a great deal from the history of stock market disasters, including timeless lessons about investing. The main conclusion includes controlling risks, doing extensive research, grasping market fundamentals, and keeping an eye on technological improvements. These classes will provide students with the knowledge they need to construct a solid investment strategy and successfully navigate the volatile stock market as they start into the world of finance.

The Role of Speculation in the Stock Market

Introduction

The stock market is essential to our global economy and is frequently portrayed as an ecosystem of financial activity. Here, investors purchase and sell company shares in the hopes of increasing their wealth and making profits. Speculation is one of the major forces affecting stock prices among the many other reasons. We shall examine the function of speculation in the stock market in the following paragraphs with the goal of helping students understand this idea.

Understanding Speculation

In simple terms, speculation is the practice of making financial decisions based more on speculation about future market movements than on a thorough evaluation of the performance of a company. In contrast to long-term investing, which means buying assets with the goal of holding them for a long time, speculation means grabbing the opportunity presented by brief market swings.

Speculators in the Stock Market

There are many different kinds of speculators, from small-time traders to major institutional investors. For example, day traders purchase and sell stocks in a single trading day with the goal of making money off of intraday price changes. Institutional investors, including hedge funds, can also engage in speculative activity, utilizing complex tactics to profit from temporary market patterns.

The Reasons for Speculation

The motivations driving speculation are diverse.The thrill of short-term trading and its potential for rapid gains attract certain individuals. Some might try to profit from opportunistic possibilities in the market or protect themselves from risks. Compared to long-term investing, speculating has a higher degree of risk, even though it can result in significant profits.

Impact on Market Dynamics

Speculation has a significant effect on the stock market's general dynamics. Speculators' continuous buying and selling ads to market liquidity, which facilitates trade execution for investors. Excessive speculation, however, can also result in more market volatility since mood and speculation may influence short-term changes more strongly than underlying economic fundamentals.

Risks and Rewards of Speculation

It is important that students understand the potential hazards and benefits linked to speculation. On the one hand, profitable speculation can result in large gains, making it possible for people to become wealthy quickly. However, speculating that doesn't work out might lead to big losses. When participating in speculative activities, students should understand the value of careful study, risk management, and a disciplined approach.

Conclusion

In conclusion,To sum up, speculation is essential to the stock market's functioning and shapes short-term price fluctuations. Understanding the difference between long-term investing and speculation is essential for students as they dive deeper into the subject of finance. Even while speculating can present thrilling chances, it is crucial to proceed cautiously, stressing the significance of due diligence, minimizing risks, and a long-term outlook for long-term financial success in the stock market.

Stock Market Indexes: A Guide for Young Investors

Young investors need not be scared by what may appear to be a mysterious and adventurous entry into the stock market! Consider the stock market to be a playground with slides and swings, and the firms to be the playing cards of friends. We have superhero teams known as "Stock Market Indexes" to help us make sense of this enormous playground. We'll explain all of this in plain English in this book for you, the aspiring financial explorers.

Understanding the Jungle

Similar to a jungle, the stock market is full with thousands of businesses that are either flourishing on vines of prosperity or falling into the bushes of losses. Our superhero guides, indexes, enable us in navigating this dangerous landscape. Similar businesses are grouped together, such as those that make interesting playlists for various musical genres.

Meet the VIPs – Indexes

The cool kids' club of the stock market is an index. Consider them as special VIP areas, to which only the most valuable and attractive businesses are granted entry. They are available in several forms, such as the "Market Cap Index," which classifies businesses according to size, ranging from giants to losers. Additionally, there is the "Sector Index," where businesses that perform identical duties group together like best friends.

Decoding the Index Mystery

You may wonder what an index is. It's similar to a DJ's playlist, except with stocks instead! These playlists support understanding of the top businesses in the industry. Some indexes employ a mathematical technique known as "weighted averages," in which larger companies—the louder friends—get more attention at the gathering.

Become an Explorer in the Stock Market

Why are indexes helpful for you? For that reason, they resemble treasure maps in the stock market. Simply check the index to find out how well the market, or the jungle, is doing. It informs us about the general happiness or sad atmosphere of the celebration. Indexes also enable us to observe trends: are digital businesses now taking center stage, or is the healthcare industry finally making a comeback?

You and other young investors have access to an excellent tool known as index funds. These represent golden tickets to the celebration of the stock market. You don't have to worry about choosing the best companies to invest in when you use index funds to hold a portion of each one on the playlist. It's like having a small taste of each flavor of ice cream; even if you don't like one, you could like another.

Final Thought

Indexes are your road maps through the exciting twists and turns of the stock market. So, prepare for a daring adventure into the heart of the financial jungle by putting on your explorer's helmet, grabbing your binoculars, and getting ready, young investor. Your trustworthy friends on this thrilling journey are the indexes.

Understanding Dividends

Introduction

In the worlds of investment and finance, dividends are vital. Gaining understanding of dividends and their significance is a crucial step towards financial literacy for students stepping into the complicated world of personal finance. Dividends are essentially the sum of a company's profits given to its shareholders. Through an explanation of their workings and an analysis of their importance, this piece seeks to clarify the concept of dividends.

Understanding Dividends

Fundamentally, a dividend is an award that a business gives to its shareholders. Purchasing shares in a company effectively makes you a co-owner. A percentage of the company's profits, which are given out as dividends, are yours as a shareholder. While some companies may pay dividends monthly or annually, many companies pay them quarterly.

How Dividends Work

Assume you are a shareholder of XYZ Ltd., a hypothetical firm. Through its operations, this company makes money. XYZ Ltd. chooses to distribute some of these profits to its shareholders rather than reinvested in the company. The board of directors of a company announces a dividend and specifies the payout amount per share. The shareholders are subsequently paid this dividend.

It's crucial to remember that not every business pays dividends. While some companies choose to give a portion of their revenues to shareholders, others choose to reinvest all of their profits to support business growth. Investors frequently select growth stocks or dividend-paying companies according to their risk tolerance and financial objectives.

Why Dividends Matter

1.Income Generation

Dividends can give students a reliable source of money. For people who are making long-term investments, like creating a retirement fund or saving for education, this income can be quite beneficial.

2.Stability and Predictability

Stocks that pay dividends are frequently linked to reliable, established businesses. These businesses have a track record of steady profit-making, thus their dividend payments are largely predictable. Investors may find this predictability comforting, particularly in periods of market instability.

3.Compounding Effect

Investing in dividends can result in the compounding effect, which raises your investment by the more shares you buy with the dividends you have reinvested in addition to the stock price appreciation. This compounding can increase your overall returns dramatically over time.

4.Alignment of Interests

A company's decision to pay dividends conveys to investors the management's assurance in the business's financial stability. A company's stock performance may benefit from the trust and transparency that this alignment of interests between shareholders and management promotes.

Considerations for Students

Although dividends can be a useful part of an investment plan, there are a few important things that students should know. First off, not all stocks that pay dividends are made equal, so before making an investment, you should always check a company's financial standing.Additionally, diversification is key to managing risk, so spreading investments across different sectors and industries can help mitigate potential losses.

Conclusion

In conclusion,understanding dividends and their significance is a critical first step for students navigating the world of finances. In addition to being a reliable source of income, dividends also give investors security, compounding opportunities, and a means of aligning their interests with those of the firms they invest in. Students may make wise investing decisions and put themselves on the path to financial success by understanding the fundamentals of dividends.

The Impact of Economic Indicators on Stocks

First of all,

It might seem like a difficult undertaking to understand the stock market, particularly for students who are just beginning to learn about the field of finance. However, one important factor that significantly shapes stock market patterns is the impact of economic indicators. Economic indicators are measures or signals that shed light on the state and functioning of an economy. This piece seeks to explain to students, in an approachable and clear manner, how these factors affect stocks.

1. Gross Domestic Product (GDP)

GDP, or gross domestic product, is one of the most basic economic metrics. Consider GDP to be the total rupee amount of all goods and services generated inside the boundaries of a nation. A robust and rising economy is indicated by an increasing GDP. Companies are probably going to see larger earnings during these times, which will raise the price of their stock. Conversely, a declining GDP could be an indication of economic problems, which would lead investors to sell their stocks, which would lower the price.

2. Rate of Unemployment

The state of employment in a nation has a big impact on stock prices. The fraction of the workforce without a job is represented by the unemployment rate. Reduced consumer spending due to high unemployment might affect business profits and, in turn, stock prices. On the other hand, a low unemployment rate denotes a robust labor market, which generally raises stock prices and consumer confidence.

3. Inflation

The general increase in the cost of goods and services, known as inflation, can have a significant effect on stock prices. In general, moderate inflation is regarded as beneficial to an economy. On the other hand, rising inflation might result in higher interest rates and reduce customers' purchasing power. Companies may find borrowing more costly as a result of rising interest rates, which might have an adverse effect on their profitability and lower stock prices.

4. Rates of Interest

Central banks establish interest rates that affect the cost of borrowing for both consumers and companies. Companies find it less expensive to borrow money for expansion when interest rates are low, which boosts investment and raises stock values. On the other hand, increasing interest rates may result in more borrowing costs, which may restrict economic expansion and lower stock prices.

5. Consumer Confidence

Consumer sentiment is a key factor in the state of the economy. People prefer to spend more when they feel optimistic about the state of the economy, which raises stock prices and company earnings. Conversely, a drop in consumer confidence may result in lower spending, which could have an impact on business profits and lower stock prices.

Conclusion

The dynamic and interconnected web that forms the financial landscape is the relationship between stocks and economic indicators. Knowing these signs can help students who are just starting out in the investment world gain important insights into the factors that affect stock prices. Every statistic, including GDP growth, employment, inflation, interest rates, and consumer confidence, influences the rise and fall of the stock market. Students who understand these ideas will be better equipped to navigate the complex financial world and make sound choices. As you start your journey into the stock market, a solid understanding of economic indicators will serve you as a compass, guiding you through the ever-changing landscape of finance.

A Guide to Understanding the Dynamics of Stock Splits

First of all,

For students exploring the particulars of the Indian stock market, the concept of stock splits is a significant component that requires consideration. We're going to understand stock splits in the Indian context in this piece.

1. Defining Stock Splits in India

The basic idea of a stock split in India is the same as it is everywhere else: it divides an existing share base into several new shares. In this division, stockholders receive a specific number of additional shares for each share they currently possess. This division is indicated through a ratio, such as 2-for-1 or 5-for-1.

2. Affordability and Market Accessibility

To make their shares more affordable is one of the main reasons Indian companies choose to split their stocks. A high price per share may prevent small investors from participating. Companies hope to draw in a wider range of investors by lowering the price of individual shares through a stock split, which will increase market accessibility.

3. The Impact on Shareholders

In India, the effect on current shareholders is proportionate to the stock split ratio, much like in the rest of the world. For example, in a 2-for-1 split, each share that a shareholder already owns is split into another share. The overall value of their investment stays constant even if the number of shares rises.

4. Market Perception and Confidence

A stock split can be interpreted as a good sign. It frequently implies that the business is financially sound and plans to expand in the future. By letting the market know that the company is confident in its future, the move to split shares may increase investor confidence.

5. Reverse Stock Splits in India

Conversely, companies might also think about reverse stock splits, especially if their share prices are extremely low. In a reverse split, the number of shares is decreased while their individual value is increased by consolidating the existing shares. Usually, this move is made in order to fulfill the minimum share price requirements for stock exchange listings.

6. Historical Context and Examples

Examining historical examples can help students understand stock splits in India better. For example, they may look into examples where well-known Indian companies chose to divide their stocks and analyze how the market responded. This practical method can offer insightful information about the practical effects of stock splits.

Conclusion

To sum up, students navigating the stock market need to understand stock splits as part of their financial literacy. The reasons for stock splits in India are consistent with worldwide patterns; they are centered around improving market accessibility and indicating strong business performance. The understanding of stock splits provides students with an invaluable instrument to analyze market dynamics and arrive at well-informed investing selections within the stock market, as their grasp of financial conditions expands.

The Psychology of Successful Stock Investors

First of all,

Stock market investing may be an exciting but difficult activity. Although success requires a solid grasp of financial markets and economic trends, investor psychology is a critical factor. In addition to understanding all aspects of financial markets, successful stock investors are skilled at controlling their emotions and coming to logical conclusions. We will examine the psychological factors in this piece that help stock investors succeed, offering insightful information to students who are just starting out in the financial markets.

1. Emotional stability and risk tolerance:

Profitable stock investors understand how much risk they can take. They are aware of the inherent volatility and swings in the stock market. It's critical to have emotional stability despite market fluctuations.

When they enter the investing world, students need to be realistic about how much risk they can take. Fear and greed are two examples of emotions that may hinder judgment and cause inappropriate judgments. As a result, to successfully navigate the inevitable highs and lows of the market, successful investors develop emotional resilience.

2. Long-Term Vision and Patience:

The most prosperous investors take a long-term outlook. They keep their eyes on the bigger picture and acknowledge that brief market swings are a part of the trip. Instead of giving in to the temptation of quick money, students should learn to have the patience necessary to ride out market storms. Wealthy investors recognize that building wealth through stocks is a journey, not a race. Despite brief failures, they are able to stick to their financial strategy thanks to this mentality.

3. Decision-Making and Information Processing:

Information is widely available and readily accessible in the digital era. Experienced investors are adept at sorting through this enormous amount of data and arriving at well-informed conclusions. They are aware of whether to believe statistics and when to follow their gut. Students should refine their critical thinking abilities to distinguish between accurate and false information. Furthermore, wise investors recognize that achieving flawless timing in the stock market is unrealistic and that making well-informed selections holds greater significance than trying to time it precisely.

4. Continuous Learning and Adaptability:

The stock market is dynamic and subject to many influences, including changes in the economy, world politics, and technology. Successful investors are lifelong learners who constantly add to their body of knowledge. In order to stay aware of market developments and modify their investment strategies accordingly, students should adopt an attitude of perpetual learning. One essential quality that helps investors effectively handle shifting market situations is flexibility.

5. Diversification and Risk Management:

A key component of investment strategy is diversification. To reduce risk, experienced investors diversify their holdings across a variety of asset classes. It is important for students to know the value of diversity and to not put all of their eggs in one basket. In addition, effective risk management is a necessary component of profitable investing. To guard against large losses on their portfolios, investors employ instruments like stop-loss orders and clearly defined risk parameters.

Conclusion:

To sum up, the psychology of profitable stock investors combines strategic thinking, emotional intelligence, and ongoing learning. When students begin their financial travels, they should realize how important it is to develop mental stability, understand their personal risk tolerance, and have a long-term outlook. Success in the ever-changing world of stock investing. It also depends on having the capacity to handle information efficiently, adjust to shifting market conditions, and put sensible risk management techniques into practice. Through the acquisition of these psychological skills, students can establish the groundwork for a fulfilling and enduring investment journey.

The Significance of Technical Analysis in Stock Market Decision-Making

A key instrument for assisting investors in navigating the complexities of the stock market is technical analysis. It is a technique that uses past price and trading volume data to assess and forecast future price movements. Technical analysis is significant because it may help investors make well-informed decisions by offering insightful information about market patterns, pointing out possible entry and exit opportunities, and more.

The focus that technical analysis places on examining price charts and patterns is one of its main features. Head and shoulders, double tops or bottoms, and triangles are examples of chart patterns that can be used to visualize market emotion and possible trend changes. Investors can predict future price changes and modify their investment strategy by identifying these trends. Even individuals who are unfamiliar with investing can understand market data more easily thanks to this visual method.

Moreover, technical analysis helps investors identify crucial support and resistance levels. Support levels represent price points where a stock historically tends to stop declining, while resistance levels indicate where it faces obstacles in rising further. Understanding these levels aids investors in making well-timed buy or sell decisions, contributing to the overall success of their investment endeavors.

Using technical indicators is a crucial aspect of technical analysis. Quantitative evaluations of a stock's momentum, overbought or oversold circumstances, and other important factors can be obtained through indicators like stochastic oscillators, moving averages, and the relative strength index (RSI). These indicators provide insightful hints to help investors make choices that are consistent with market trends, risk tolerance, and investment objectives.

Technical analysis is also a crucial instrument for risk management. Investors can determine the possible risks connected to a specific investment by evaluating past price volatility and trends. They can put tactics like stop-loss orders into place thanks to this risk-aware strategy, shielding their investments from unforeseen market swings.

It's critical to make decisions quickly in the volatile and fast-paced stock market. Technical analysis gives investors a methodical and disciplined way to quickly analyze market data. It gives them the ability to quickly take advantage of opportunities, recognize new trends, and adjust to shifting market conditions.

In conclusion, it is impossible to exaggerate the significance of technical analysis in stock market decision-making. It gives investors the resources they need to examine past data, spot patterns and trends, and decide whether to purchase or sell. Investors can improve their ability to understand the complexities of the stock market and raise their chances of reaching their financial objectives by implementing technical analysis into their investment plans.

53

18 Technical Ratios

1. Price-to-Earnings Ratio (P/E)

Let's break down the Price-to-Earnings Ratio (P/E) in an easy way for YOU!

Imagine you and your friends are running lemonade stands. The Price-to-Earnings Ratio is like a simple way to figure out how much people are willing to pay for a cup of lemonade compared to how much money each stand is making.

This is how you understand it:

1. Lemonade Price (P):
   - This is the cost that customers are paying at each stand for a cup of lemonade. See it as the "price tag" attached to the lemonade.

2. Profits (E):

- This is the entire income or profit as it is known in the context of lemonade stands. It's similar to calculating how much money is left over after deducting the cost of producing the lemonade.

3. P/E Ratio:

- This P/E Ratio is now a basic math problem. You divide the Earnings (E) by the Price of Lemonade (P). It's comparable to asking, "How many times the lemonade price is compared to how much money each stand is making?"

Example: - Let's say Stand A sells lemonade for $2 a cup, and after subtracting all the costs, it makes $1 in profit. The P/E Ratio would be 2 (price) divided by 1 (earnings), which equals 2.

What Does It Mean?

- If the P/E Ratio is high (say, 20 or more), it may indicate that consumers are prepared to pay a premium for a cup of lemonade in relation to the revenue generated by the stand. This could indicate that investors believe there is a great deal of room for future profit-making on the stand.

A low P/E ratio (less than or equal to 5) may indicate that consumers are not prepared to pay much for a cup of lemonade in relation to the profit. This may imply that investors are not expecting significant growth or profits from the stand.

In summary, the Price-to-Earnings Ratio provides insight into how much people value a company based on its actual earnings rather than its perceived worth. It's similar to determining whether or not consumers are prepared to spend more for the lemonade because they think it will be very popular!

While,it is only one aspect of P/E ratio but there are many.It is also used to determine whether the stock is overvalued or undervalued based on Market P/E. Again, it is only one of the aspects of this ratio.

2. Earnings per Share (EPS)

Okay, let's start a basic explanation of earnings per share (EPS):

Let's say you and your brothers decide to launch a small company selling handcrafted goods. Calculating earnings per share (EPS) is similar to calculating the profit margin for each friend in a firm when multiple friends are involved.

This is how you interpret it:

1. Profit (Earnings)

This is the whole profit your tiny company makes. It's similar to adding up all of the proceeds from sales of your handmade goods after deducting the cost of production.

2. The total number of shares (friends)

"Shares" in the context of business refer to portions or ownership stakes. The entire number of friends who contributed to the firm is represented by the number of shares.

3. Earnings per Share (EPS)

You now divide the total Earnings by the number of Shares to determine the profit each friend made. It's comparable to stating, "If we share all the profit equally among ourselves, how much does each friend get?"

As an example:

Assume that your company earned $100 in profit and that you have 10 friends who own shares in it. $100 in earnings would be divided by 10 shares to get $10 in earnings per share, or EPS.

What Does It Mean? - A high earnings per share (say, $10 or more) indicates that each buddy receives a larger portion of the profit and that the company is earning a respectable amount per share.

- Each buddy will receive a lower portion of the profit if the Earnings per Share is low, such as $1 or less, and the company may not be as profitable per share.

Thus, earnings per share helps in our understanding of the profit that each "share" of ownership stake in a company receives. It's a means of analyzing the success of the enterprise for every individual associated.

3. Price/Earnings to Growth (PEG) Ratio

Let's understand the Price/Earnings to Growth (PEG) Ratio in simple words

1. The ratio of price to earnings (P/E)

Prior to going into PEG, let us recall P/E. How much consumers are ready to pay for a company's earnings is shown by the P/E ratio. It's similar to determining whether a video game is worth purchasing by comparing its cost against its enjoyment.

2. Growth in Earnings:

Let's now consider a game that improves with time. Saying "How fast is this game getting more fun, and how much more money is it making?" is what earnings growth is like.

4. PEG Ratio

- PEG Ratio integrates the two. It's equivalent to comparing a game's price (P/E) to its increasing quality and enjoyment (Earnings Growth). To calculate PEG, divide P/E by earnings growth.

As an example:

Consider a game with a $20 (P) price and a 10 P/E ratio. In other words, people are paying ten times what they make. The PEG Ratio would be 10 (P/E) divided by 20 (Earnings Growth), or 0.5, if the game is becoming, let's say, 20% more enjoyable annually (i.e., earnings growth of 20%).

What Does That Signify? - The game (or stock) may be a good deal if the PEG Ratio is low, such as 1 or below. For the growth in earnings, people are not paying very much. It's similar to purchasing a game at a fair price that is constantly growing better.

- A high PEG ratio (such as 2 or more) indicates that consumers may be paying a higher price for the anticipated growth. It's similar to spending a lot of money on a game that's becoming better, but you have to decide if the increased cost is justified.

In conclusion, the PEG Ratio is a useful tool for determining whether consumers are paying a reasonable price for a company's anticipated growth, much like it is for determining whether a video game is worth its price in relation to its ongoing improvements.

5. Dividend Yield

Let's break down Dividend Yield in an easy way

Assume you pay $100 for each share of a company. This company distributes dividends to its owners as a means of distributing its earnings. Suppose there is a $5 annual dividend per share.

Let's calculate the dividend yield now:

Dividend Yield is calculated as (Average Annual Dividend / Stock Price) x 100.

Here, it would be as follows:

Dividend Yield = ($5 / $100) x 100 = 5%

Thus, 5% is the dividend yield.

This implies that you will receive $5 in dividend payments annually for every $100 you invested in the company's stock. It resembles a percentage return on investment that is determined by the dividends you get.

Let's now contrast this with a different company. Let's say you discover another stock that is valued at $200 per share and yields $10 in dividends every year.

($10 / $200) x 100 = 5% is the dividend yield.

The dividend yield is still 5% even though the stock price and payout amount have increased. This is simply a result of receiving more dividends despite paying more for the stock.

To sum up, dividend yield is a measurement that allows you to calculate the annual return on your stock investment based on the dividends that the company pays out. It aids investors in comparing the possible revenue from various equities, independent of the stocks' actual prices.

6. Price-to-Book Ratio (P/B)

1. What is a Book Value?

- A company's "book value" can be defined as its net worth, which is the sum of its assets less its liabilities.

2. P/B Ratio Definition

- The Price-to-Book Ratio (P/B) shows how a company's book value compares to what the market is willing to pay. It is similar to comparing a company's stock market price to the information included in its financial "book."

3. P/B Ratio Formula

This is an easy formula to use: Market Value per share/ Book Value per share.

4. P/B Ratio Interpretation:

A company with a P/B ratio of 1 indicates that its book value is precisely what the market is willing to pay. Investors are prepared to pay the full book value of the company.

- The market values the company less than its book value if the P/B ratio is less than 1, It might qualify as a "discount."

- The market values the company more than its book value if the P/B ratio is greater than 1, Investors are prepared to spend more.

5. Example:

Assume that a company's stock is trading at $20 per share, but its book value is just $10 per share.
   - It would be 20/10=2 for the P/B ratio.
   - This indicates that investors are prepared to buy shares at a price twice the book value.

6. Thoughts:

A stock may not always be a good value just because its P/B ratio is low. It can indicate that there are problems with the business that the market is worried about.

- In the same manner, a high P/B ratio does not always indicate an expensive stock. It could imply that investors anticipate continued excellent performance.

In Summary

P/B Ratio is equivalent to comparing a company's stock market price with the value stated in its financial records. It aids investors in determining if a stock is selling at a premium or at a discount to book value.

7. Return on Equity (ROE)

1. What is Equity?

- Equity can be thought of as the shareholders' portion of a company's ownership. It is the amount that, in theory, would remain for shareholders in the event that the business sold all of its assets and settled all of its debts.

2. What is Return on Equity (ROE)?

- Return on Equity (ROE) is a metric used to assess how effectively a business uses the equity of its shareholders to produce profits.

3. ROE Calculation

- ROE has a straightforward formula:

Net Income/Shareholders' Equity multiply by 100%

- It's equivalent to asking, "How much money is the company making for every dollar of shareholders' equity?" to put it even more simply.

4. Understanding ROE

- A company with a 15% ROE is making $0.15 (or 15 cents) in profit for each dollar of equity that shareholders possess.
   - A higher ROE typically indicates that the business is making profitable use of its equity.

5. Example

- Assume that a business has $10 million shareholders' equity and a $1 million net income.

The ROE would be 1,000,000/10,000,000 multiply by 100% = 10%

- This means the company is earning a 10% return on the equity invested by its shareholders.

- ROE is like a report card that tells you how well a company is turning the money invested by its owners (shareholders) into profits.

- It helps investors understand the efficiency and profitability of a company in using its shareholders' equity.

8. Debt-to-Equity Ratio

A financial metric called the debt-to-equity ratio aids in our understanding of how a company maintains its operations and investments. Let's simplify it so that pupils can understand it:

Debt-to-Equity Ratio = Total Debt / Shareholders' Equity

- Total Debt: This covers everything of a company's debt, including bonds and loans.

- Shareholders' Equity: This is a representation of the funds that the company's owners, or shareholders, own. The retained profits and common stock are among its contents.

Now consider the ratio as a means of observing the balance between the amount of money that a business has borrowed (debt) and the amount of money that its owners have invested (equity).

What the Ratio Indicates:

- If the ratio is low (less than 1), it means the business depends more on the capital of its owners than it does on loans. Given that the business is not overly indebted, this may indicate stability in its finances.

- A ratio that is high (more than 1) indicates that the company's debt to equity ratio is higher. Due to its substantial debt, the business may be exposed to increased financial risk.

- If the ratio is 1, the company's debt and equity amounts are equal. One could consider this to be a balanced scenario.

Example

Suppose the company has $1 billion in shareholders' equity and $500 million in total debt.

$500 million / $1 billion = 0.5 is the debt-to-equity ratio.

Since the ratio in this case is 0.5, the corporation has more equity than debt.

Recall that how the ratio should be interpreted varies depending on the sector and unique conditions of the company. An industry-specific ratio might not be appropriate for another. For a more insightful study, ratios should always be compared to competitors' or the industry average.

9. Current Ratio

Consider that you have a friend who enjoys collecting toys and action figures. Let's take an example where your friend asks you if you have enough money to pay for his immediate needs, such as replacing any broken action figures or purchasing new ones

1. Current Assets

In the stock market, the current ratio is comparable to determining whether a buddy has enough liquid assets (cash or readily marketable goods) to meet his immediate demands.

2. Present Resources

Consider everything your friend possesses that he can easily sell for money if necessary. This may be his piggy bank, his wallet, or any action figures he's prepared to part with fast

3. Current Liability

These are the immediate expenses that your friend must cover. It might be any short-term debts he has, such as money he owes someone for purchasing a new action figure.

This is how the current ratio is now calculated:

Current Ratio= Current Liability/Current Assets

Put simply, it indicates the number of times your friend can use his assets that can be easily converted into cash to pay for his immediate needs.

In simple terms, it tells you how many times your friend can cover his short-term expenses with the things he owns that can be quickly turned into cash.

For example, if your friend has $200 worth of action figures he can quickly sell and he owes $100 to others, his current ratio would be 200/100=2

With a current ratio of 2, he has twice as many assets as he needs to pay off his current debts.

Investors in the stock market use a company's current ratio to evaluate its short-term financial standing. More current assets to cover short-term commitments is indicated by a larger current ratio, which is generally regarded as positive. It's similar to making sure your friend has an adequate supply of action figures that he can sell fast to pay for his immediate needs!

10. Enterprise Value

Let's break down the concept of enterprise value in a simple way:

Let's say you wish to purchase a lemonade stand.The price you agree to pay for the stand is like the market value of the entire business, right? However, there's more to think about. As part of the agreement, the seller may have some debt (money borrowed) or cash on hand.

Nowadays, considering enterprise value is similar to adopting a new viewpoint when examining the lemonade stand. Rather of concentrating solely on the asking price, you additionally take into account the amount of debt (money the company owes) and cash (money the company possesses). This provides you with a more accurate understanding of the true cost of owning the whole company.

So, in simple terms, enterprise value is the total cost you'd face if you wanted to buy the whole business, including its debts and considering its available cash.

In mathematics, it's frequently written as:

Enterprise Value=Market Value of Equity+Total Debt−Cash and Cash Equivalents

Investors can use it to determine a company's actual worth by taking into account both its ownership and financial commitments.

11. Market Capitalization

Let's simplify the concept of market capitalization

Let's say you decide to start a lemonade shop with your friends. You choose to divide the stand's ownership into equal portions known as shares in order to make things fair. A certain amount of shares are given to each buddy, and when all the shares are owned collectively, the lemonade stand as a whole is owned.

Let's now assume that you wish to determine the total market value of the lemonade stand. Market capitalization enters the picture here.

Finding the entire worth of each of the lemonade stand shares that would be sold in the market is similar to determining market capitalization. The computation involves multiplying the total quantity of shares by the present value of every share.

Market Capitalization=Total Number of Shares×Price per Share

So, if your lemonade stand has 100 shares, and each share is valued at $10, the market capitalization would be

100 shares×$10 per share=$1000

100 shares×$10per share=$1000.

Similar to your neighborhood lemonade stand, firms have shares on the stock market, and market capitalization gives us an idea of a company's total worth. In comparison to companies with lower market capitalization, those with higher market capitalization are typically regarded as larger or more valuable.

Note that market capitalization provides us with an estimate of the total value of the firm based on the value of its shares and is only one method of evaluating a company's size on the stock market.

In the stock market, the current ratio is comparable to determining whether a buddy has enough liquid assets (cash or readily marketable goods) to meet his immediate demands.

12. Quick Ratio (Acid-Test Ratio)

Of course! Let's make the Quick Ratio, also called the Acid-Test Ratio, easier for learners to understand:

Let's say you have a friend who stores valuable and uncommon trade cards. Let's take an example where your friend needs to know right away if he can pay for an unexpected expense, such as purchasing a just released rare card.

Comparable to determining if a buddy has enough liquid assets (cash and easily sellable items) to fulfill his short-term needs, the Quick Ratio in the stock market is a little stricter than the Current Ratio because it leaves out certain less liquid assets.

This is how it operates:

1. Quick Assets

Consider these to be your friend's most liquid possessions—items that can be easily converted into cash. This may represent to him the cash in his wallet and the easily tradable and highly sought-after trade cards.

2. Current Liabilities

These are the immediate bills your friend has to pay, such as the money he owes a third party for purchasing a new trading card.

The Quick Ratio is now computed as follows:

Quick Ratio= Current Liability/Quick Assets

For example, if your friend has $100 in his wallet and $50 worth of highly sought-after trading cards that he can quickly sell, and he owes $75 to others, his Quick Ratio would be

100+50/75=150/75= 2

With a Quick Ratio of 2, he has twice as many highly liquid assets as he needs to pay down his current debts.

Investors in the stock market use a company's Quick Ratio to determine if it can meet short-term obligations with its most liquid assets. It's similar to making sure your friend can swiftly meet his short-term needs without depending on less liquid assets by making sure he has enough cash and highly sought-after trading cards.

Difference between Current Ratio and Quick Ratio

Current Ratio:

- Takes into account all quick and not so quick assets.

- Contains everything that can be swiftly converted into cash.

Quick Ratio (Acid-Test Ratio):

- Only takes into account the assets that are most liquid.

- Does not include certain less liquid assets that could take some time to turn into cash.

In summary:

- The current ratio takes a wider range of assets into account, making it more inclusive.

The Quick Ratio highlights the most liquid assets and is more constrictive.

Analogy:

Seeing your friend's entire bank account, including coins and notes, is similar to looking at their current ratio.

Quick Ratio is similar to focusing exclusively on the bills and disregarding the coins since it may require more work to turn coins into cash.

13. Beta

Definition

A metric called beta can be used to determine how much a specific stock tends to move in proportion to the stock market as a whole.

1. Dancing Partners

- Say you are attending a dancing party. Every stock is a dancer, and the stock market is the dance floor. Beta indicates the degree to which a stock synchronizes with the whole dance floor. When the beta is 1, they are in sync. A stock dancer with a beta of less than one dances a little more cautiously, whereas one with a beta of more than one dances more energetically.

2. Ride Buddies on a Roller Coaster

- Visualize the stock market as a roller coaster with individual stocks as tiny cars.

- A stock with a beta of 1 is comparable to an automobile that precisely tracks the highs and lows of a roller coaster.

- A beta of less than one indicates that the market (the roller coaster) moves more quickly than the vehicle, or the stock. If the car overestimates the roller coaster's motions, its beta value is greater than 1.

Explanation: -

Beta = 1: The stock follows the market's movement.

Beta <1: The stock exhibits lower volatility compared to the market.

Beta > 1 indicates that the stock is more volatile than the market.

As an illustration, suppose Stock A's beta is 0.8. This would be equivalent to stating, "Stock A dances a little more gracefully than the overall dance floor."
   A beta of 1.2 for Stock B is equivalent to stating that "Stock B is an enthusiastic dancer, moving a bit more than the dance floor."

Why It Matters to Investors:

- Risk Assessment: Beta aids in educating investors about the level of risk attached to a specific asset. Greater beta might indicate increased risk as well as potential returns.

- Diversity: Beta is a tool that investors can use to diversify their holdings. To offset the total risk, they may add some low-beta equities if they have high-beta ones.

To put it briefly, beta serves as an investor's companion on a roller coaster or dance partner, indicating how closely a stock follows the market.

14. Alpha

An investor can evaluate a company or investment's performance in relation to its expected or benchmark return by looking at its alpha value.

1. Winners of Races

- Imagine a race in which every stock is a competitor and the average speed of all competitors is the expected performance.

- A stock that outperforms (or underperforms) the anticipated performance is awarded an alpha, which is similar to a trophy. The stock performed better when the alpha was positive, and worse when it was negative.

2. Grades in School

- Consider a class where the instructor has set a target for the average score. A student receives a positive mark if their score is higher than average, and a negative grade if it is lower.

- Alpha can be thought of as a stock's grade depending on how it performed in relation to expectations.

Analysis

Good Alpha:The stock outperformed expectations.

Negative Alpha: The stock underperformed relative to expectations.

Example

- Stock X has a positive alpha of +2% if it was predicted to return 8% but instead returned 10%. That did better than expected, according to this.

   - Stock Y has a negative alpha of -2% if it was predicted to return 12% but only 10% of that amount. This indicates that it fell short of expectations.

Why It is Important for Investors:

-Performance Evaluation

Alpha assists investors in assessing a stock's performance in comparison to the market or a benchmark.

- Risk-Adjusted Returns

By taking risk into account, alpha offers a more complex picture of performance than simply examining raw returns.

- Portfolio Management:

Investors utilize alpha to determine which investments to include and which to leave out of their portfolios.

To put it briefly, alpha is similar to a bonus or punishment applied to a stock according to how well it performed in relation to forecasts. When alpha is positive, it indicates success; when alpha is negative, it indicates failure. Investors can use it as a tool to determine the actual value that an investment adds—or subtracts.

15. Sharpe Ratio

A metric that aids investors in evaluating an investment's performance in relation to risk is the Sharpe Ratio.

1. School Grades (Risk-Adjusted)

- Think of investing as a subject in school, and each investment is a student.

- The Sharpe Ratio is like a grade that takes into account both the investment's performance (return) and how risky it is (volatility).

2. Scoring in a Game

Picture yourself participating in a game where you win by doing well. Similar to your ultimate score, the Sharpe Ratio also takes into account the number of hazardous choices you made to earn those points.

Components of Sharpe Ratio:

1. Return

The quantity of money you receive back from your investment.

2. Risk (Volatility)

The degree to which the value of your investment fluctuates.

Explanation

- Higher Sharpe Ratio:

A higher score (similar to a winning grade in a game or an A+ in school) signifies that the investment has produced respectable returns given the degree of risk assumed.

- Lower Sharpe Ratio:

A lower score, similar to a lower grade or score in a game, indicates that, considering its degree of risk, the investment could not be yielding enough profits.

Formula (for the curious):

Sharpe Ratio=Volatility of Investment/Return of Investment-Risk-Free Rate

Why It Matters to Investors:

- The Trade-off Between Risk and Reward:

Investors can determine whether they are receiving a sufficient return for the amount of risk they are taking by using the Sharpe Ratio.

- Evaluative Comparison:

By comparing various assets using the Sharpe Ratio, investors can determine which one provides a higher risk-adjusted return.

-Portfolio Enhancement:

Investors seek to assemble a portfolio consisting of a variety of assets that when combined yield a respectable return on risk.

To sum up, the Sharpe Ratio can be compared to an investment report card that takes into account both the investment's profitability and risk level. Examining the ratio of return to risk enables investors to make better-informed choices.

16. Relative Strength Index (RSI)

Explanation:

A useful tool for traders and investors to determine whether a company or market is oversold or overbought—a sign of a potential change in direction—is the Relative Strength Index (RSI).

1. Tug of War

Think of it as a tug-of-war between two groups. In the event that one team pulls too strongly (overbought) or too weakly (oversold), the RSI acts like a referee's whistle.

- If a team is overbought, it might be getting tired and is more likely to lose some ground. If it's oversold, it might be ready for a comeback.

2. Levels of Energy

Consider a stock as a competitor in a race. Similar to a measurement, RSI indicates the runner's level of energy and fatigue.

- The runner may require a rest if they have been sprinting for an extended period of time (overbought). They may possess the energy for a quick burst of speed if they have been overselling and jogging slowly.

Understanding

- RSI Readings:

- 70 and above: Overbought (potential for a pullback or reversal).

- 30 and below: Oversold (potential for a bounce or upward movement).

Why It Matters for Students

Timing Moves:

RSI assists students in making decisions about whether to purchase or sell stocks by assisting them in determining when a stock may be due for a change in direction.

- Indicator of Extremes

Students can determine if it would be wise to make a new investment decision by using RSI, which signals when a stock is at an extreme level.

- Easy Analysis Tool: Students are introduced to technical analysis, or the examination of stock charts, through the use of RSI, a straightforward technique.

-In the real world

A stock's RSI of 75 is equivalent to the referee stating, "Hey, this stock has been pulling hard, and it might need a breather."

A reading of 25 on the RSI is like the referee declaring, "This stock has been weak for a while, and it could be ready for a comeback."

To put it simply, the Relative Strength Index (RSI) functions as a kind of game referee, signaling to investors whether a stock is being overbought or oversold. Students studying time and decision-making in the stock market can benefit from using it.

17.Promoters' Holding

Holding of Promoters

A company in the stock market is frequently founded by a group of individuals referred to as "promoters." They often resemble the company's creators or founders. The promoters also acquire a portion of the company's shares when it goes public, which is when it sells them to the general public via the stock market.

Promoters' Holding Percentage

"Promoters' holding" describes the portion of the company's total shares that these first promoters own. If all of a company's shares were a pizza, the promoters' holdings would be the pieces that the founders still kept for themselves.

Why It's Important

Promoters' holding is important since it demonstrates the founders' level of faith in their own business. A large ownership stake by the company's promoters is a sign that they are prepared to put their own money into the business and believe it will succeed. Other investors might interpret this favorably.

Impact on Stock Prices

The stock prices may also be impacted by changes in the promoters' holdings. For instance, if promoters increase their holdings, the market may interpret this as a good signal, leading to an increase in stock prices. However, stock prices may drop if promoters begin to sell off a sizable amount of their holdings, as this could frighten investors.

In Summary

A promoter's stake is when a company's creators or founders possess a percentage of its shares. It's an indication of their level of self-assurance in their company. Investors may find it useful to take this information into account when deciding whether to purchase or sell stocks.

18.Face Value

Let's simplify the concept of share face value of shares

The initial value of stock as shown on the stock certificate is known as the face value of the stock. It is sometimes referred to as the "nominal value" or "par value." But in modern finance, face value has lost some of its significance.

Consider cutting a pizza into multiple evenly-sized slices. A stock in a company is represented by each slice. At this point, the face value is equivalent to the starting price you set for each slice when you first began selling them. Assume you determine that the face value of each slice is $10.

The quality of the ingredients, the amount of people who are actually hungry for your pizza, or even the price that other people are prepared to pay for similar slices in the pizza market can all affect the actual market worth of each slice, or share. The slice's market value is comparable to the stock's current price on the stock exchange.

The true value of a stock, or a slice of pizza, is therefore decided by what people are prepared to pay for it on the open market, even though its face value is only a starting point. When making judgments, investors focus more on the market value because it represents the current supply and demand for the stock.

In conclusion, face value is similar to a stock's original price tag, but what buyers are prepared to pay for it on the stock market determines a stock's true value.

Building a Diverse Stock Portfolio

First of all,

Investing in stocks is similar to collecting various toys, since each one has distinct qualities, advantages, and characteristics of its own. Similar to how you wouldn't want to have all of one kind of toy in your toy collection, you should have variety in your stock portfolio. A varied stock portfolio improves overall success possibilities and helps in risk management. We'll go over the fundamentals of creating a diversified stock portfolio in a style that's simple and understandable for students.

Understanding Stocks

Let's review the fundamentals of stocks before going into the world of stock portfolios. Stocks are a symbol of ownership in a business. Upon purchasing a stock, you turn into a shareholder and acquire a portion of the company. Companies sell stocks to raise capital, and investors purchase these stocks to get a piece of the company's profits.

The Importance of Diversity

Assume you are holding a fruit basket. Your entire basket is at risk if you fill it with only apples and the apple market suffers. But if you have a combination of bananas, apples, and oranges, the market for one fruit might decline, but the others might do well. This is what variety is all about. Comparably, a varied stock portfolio distributes the risk, lowering the possibility that the performance of any one stock will cause the value of your entire investment to collapse.:

1. Various Sectors

- Consider the stock market to be a large city with many neighborhoods. A distinct industry, such as technology, healthcare, finance, and so forth, is represented by each community. Invest in stocks from different industries to increase diversification. While one industry may be struggling, others may be prospering.

2. Size of the Company Matters

- There are three sizes of companies: small, medium, and huge. Small businesses, sometimes known as "small-cap," may be more risk-averse yet have greater room for growth. Big businesses, sometimes known as "large-cap," are more reliable but might not have as much room for expansion. You may balance the rewards and risks in your portfolio by combining the two.

3. Diversity in Geography:

- Geographic diversity can be advantageous for your stock portfolio, just as it might be for your toy collection, which may contain toys from all over the world. Think about making investments in international businesses. By doing this, you can shield your investments from local economic fluctuations.

4. Various Kinds of Stocks

- Different characters in a novel can be compared to stocks; some are daring and aim for rapid growth, while others are reliable and bring in a consistent revenue. Growth stocks can be riskier, but they also have a high potential for return. Although dividend stocks may rise more slowly, they do produce a consistent income. Your portfolio can be balanced by having a mix.

5. Consistent Check-ins

- Maintaining a stock portfolio is not a one-time event. It requires consistent attention, much like caring for a plant. Watch your stocks, read up on the businesses you've invested in, and be informed about market movements. You can then modify your portfolio as necessary.

In summary

Creating a varied stock portfolio is similar to assembling a well-balanced dinner; for general health, you want to have a little bit of everything. Variety improves your chances of long-term success and helps you in market storms. In other words, just as you would mix up your favorite song or toy collection, make sure your stock portfolio has a well-balanced assortment of various stocks. Recall that having the appropriate combination of stocks is just as important to success as having them. Happy making purchases!

How to Research and Analyze Stocks

It's similar to knowing how to look into and select the best ingredients for your favorite cuisine to know how to explore and evaluate stocks. You can choose the companies you want to invest in by considering a number of factors. Let's simplify the procedure into a few simple steps:

1. Business Fundamentals

- Find out as much as you can about the business that interests you. How do they go about things? Are they an IT firm, a medical facility, or maybe a clothes line? It's similar to knowing what the key component in your dish is.

2. Financial Statements

- Consider financial statements as the ingredients and measures list for a dish. Financial statements such as the cash flow statement, balance sheet, and income statement of companies are available. These records provide information about the company's earnings, expenses, and savings. Keep an eye out for patterns and confirm the company's financial stability.

3. Revenue and Earnings

- Consider that you are baking a cake. You're interested in finding out who will find it enjoyable. In the same way, you want to find out if a business is profitable (earnings) and how much it is generating (revenue). Revenue and earnings growth are typically positive indicators.

4. Competitive Environment

- You should be aware of the competitors of the business, just as you could look at what other chefs are producing. Examine the company's level of differentiation within its industry. Is it the leader, or does it have fierce rivalry?

5. Team Management

- Think of the management group as the food chefs. Who is in charge of the business, and what is their reputation? Examine their background and previous decisions that they made.

6. News and Events

- Keep up with the most recent information regarding the business. Any major updates or announcements may have a substantial effect on the stock price. It's similar to keeping an eye out for fresh components that could change your dish.

7. Risks

- There are potential dangers in any recipe. All investments have some level of risk. Determine the potential problems for the business you are researching. Exist any internal problems, industrial difficulties, or economic factors that could have an impact on its success?

8. Share Buybacks and Dividends

- Certain companies distribute their profits to shareholders in the form of dividends or share buybacks. It is similar to receiving a slice of cake.

Verify whether the business you are considering follows this policy.

9. History of Stock Prices

- Examine the stock price history of the company, much like you would a restaurant's reviews. Has the stock increased steadily throughout the years, or has it previously experienced extreme swings?

10. Personal Views of the Analyst

As you would seek advice on a new eatery, see what analysts have to say about the stock. Analysts research businesses and make suggestions. Take note of their observations, but never forget that it's wise to establish your own conclusions.

11. Long-Term Perspective

- Investing is all about the long term, much like slow cooking. Examine whether the company's business plan is sufficiently robust to withstand challenges in the future.

In conclusion,

You can approach the process of studying and analyzing stocks like you would cook a well-planned dish. Recall that, just like a chef experimenting with different cuisines, your investment approach could need to be modified in accordance with your results and evolving market conditions.

The Pros and Cons of Day Trading

What is day trading?

Buying and selling financial instruments, such as stocks, currencies, or commodities, inside the same trading day is known as day trading in the financial markets. The aim of day trading is to make money on intraday volatility and short-term price fluctuations.

The advantages of day trading

1. A Chance to Make Quick Profits

Buying and selling financial products on the same day is known as day trading. This implies that you might be able to turn a profit quickly.

2. Self-reliance

For people who prefer to manage their own time and make their own decisions, day traders may find their frequent independence fascinating.

3. Educational Possibilities

It gives traders practical experience in the financial markets and aids with their understanding of market trends, patterns, and tactics.

4. No Overnight danger

Day traders minimize the danger of unexpected market swings when they're not actively trading by not holding positions overnight.

The drawbacks of day trading

1. Risky

There's a high risk associated with the possibility of quick rewards. Financial market prices are vulnerable to volatility, and day traders may suffer substantial losses.

2. Intense

It might be frustrating to constantly monitor market changes when day trading. Not everyone may be able to take it, particularly those who are under a lot of stress.

3. Lack of Time

Day trading demands commitment and time to be successful. Traders must be able to quickly assess information, stay up to date on market developments, and analyze data.

4. Costs and Fees

Day trading sometimes entails a large number of transactions, which raises the fees and costs related to trading platforms and market data.

It's important that students understand that day trading involves risk management, discipline, and a solid grasp of financial markets. It's also not an easy way to generate money. It's usually a good idea to start small and build up experience over time.

The Importance of Patience in Stock Investing

Purchasing stocks is comparable to sowing seeds in a garden. The sunshine and water that enable those seeds to sprout into robust, healthy plants is patience. Patience is an essential trait in the area of stock investing that can have a big impact on an investor's performance. Let's examine the importance of patience and how it affects students' stock investing.

1. Gaining Knowledge of the Stock Market Process

The movement of stock prices is not linear. They may rise or fall for a variety of reasons, frequently driven by temporary elements such as news, market mood, or economic developments. Being patient means knowing that investing in stocks involves ups and downs and success is measured over the long term.

2. Compound Growth's Power

Compound growth is one of the amazing advantages of investing with patience. This implies that if your investments increase in value, they may produce returns, and those returns may produce yet greater returns. It resembles a snowball sliding down a hill, only with time it gets bigger and quicker. By being patient, you can take advantage of the compounding effect, which over time can greatly boost your wealth.

3. The Purchase and Hold Approach

A crucial element of the "buy and hold" approach is patience. Long-term investors patiently hang onto their investments through market swings as compared to purchasing and selling stocks on a regular basis based on short-term market movements. This approach is predicated on the idea that the market will eventually increase and that, overall, short-term swings will become less significant.

4. Managing Volatility in the Market

Investors that possess patience are better able to withstand market volatility. Prices might fluctuate and markets can be unpredictable. During these swings, patience enables investors to maintain composure and steer clear of rash actions that might harm their long-term financial objectives.

5. Steer clear of rash decisions

Impulsive decisions, such panic selling in a market collapse or following the newest hot stock, might result from impatience. Investors that possess patience are better able to stick to their initial investing strategy and avoid making quick decisions that could backfire.

6. Realistic Expectations Setting

Being patient starts with having reasonable expectations. Students should be aware that stock investment entails risk and that results could not appear right away. Investing in the stock market to increase money is a slow and patient process.

7. Gradual Participation and Adjustment

Investing is a learning and adaptation experience. Students that exhibit patience will eventually be able to comprehend the intricacies of the market, draw lessons from their mistakes, and modify their approach.

8. Final Thoughts: The Benefits of Patience in the Long Run

In conclusion, it is impossible to exaggerate the value of patience while investing in stocks. Long-term success requires patience, which enables investors to weather market volatility and capitalize on the growth potential of their assets. PATIENT INVESTORS frequently reap the benefits of their patience over time in the form of wealth growth and financial security, much like a well-kept garden produces a plentiful harvest.

The Importance of Financial Literacy for Young People

1. Handling Money

The ability to handle money like a superhero is what financial literacy is all about. It assists you in learning how to manage your finances, including how much to spend, save, and perhaps even invest. It's similar to having a financial strategy!

2. Making Wise Decisions

Making wise financial decisions is a sign of financial literacy. It involves understanding the difference between wants and needs, or necessities and desirables. This superpower aids in budgeting and helps you stay away from impulsive purchases.

3. Preventing Financial Errors

Consider your financial literacy as a shield that keeps you safe from financial errors. You'll be able to prevent problems like overspending or falling for misleading financial schemes. It's similar to having a guide to assist you in making sound financial choices.

4. Making Future Plans

Understanding finance is like having a treasure map for the future. You'll discover how to make plans and save money for the things you truly desire, such as a car purchase, college tuition, or even opening your own company. It's all about preparing for the thrilling journeys that lie ahead!

5. Getting to Know Monetary Terms

Acquiring financial literacy is comparable to picking up a new language—the language of finances. Words like investment, credit score, budget, and interest will all make sense to you. It's similar to deciphering the financial industry's hidden code!

6. Developing confidence

Having sound financial management skills instills confidence. You'll have a greater sense of financial control and be more equipped to handle any challenge that may arise. Like a superhero, financial knowledge gives you the courage to make smart financial decisions.

7. Assisting Others

You can assist your friends and family when you have a solid understanding of financial matters. You'll become the go-to person for financial guidance, imparting your financial superpowers to others and improving their quality of life in the process.

8. Getting Ready for Achievement

To succeed, financial literacy is similar to attending a superhero training camp. It gives you the tools you need to realize your aspirations. The secret to realizing your superpotential is financial literacy, whether your goal is to launch your dream business, tour the world, or buy a house!

To put it simply, financial literacy is your superpower for managing finances sensibly, making informed decisions, and setting yourself up for future success. It is the toolkit that gives you the confidence to go through the thrilling process of handling your money and realizing your goals.

The Power of Compounding in Long-Term Investing

1. Visualize Your Cash Developing Like a Plant with Magic

Consider your money to be a magical plant. A seed is your initial investment that sprouts when it is planted. The amazing thing is that, in addition to growing, the plant also generates new seeds.

2. Magic Growth Is Similar To Compounding

Compounding is the secret to rapid money growth. It's similar to a plant that, as it grows, produces an increasing number of seeds. Compounding creates a dynamic cycle of growth where your money produces returns, and those returns generate additional returns.

3. The Process of Compounding

Assume for a moment that you invest some money and it generates a profit or interest. You now reinvest that return together with your initial investment rather than simply keeping it. The next time your money increases, it will grow on the complete amount (original + returns) rather than simply the initial amount. After repeating this pattern, the growth begins to multiply.

4. The Longer, the Better

Compounding gains greater strength the longer your money has to grow. It's like the annual growth in height and seed production of the miracle plant. Investing early is great because it gives your money more time to undergo the amazing process of compound interest.

5. Real-Life Example

Assume you make a financial investment in the stock market. It grows at an average pace throughout time. You get returns on your initial investment throughout the first year. You receive returns on the entire amount (original plus first year returns) in the second year, and so forth. Because of the miracle of compounding, your money grows more quickly as the years pass.

6. The Secret Is Patience

With time, compounding's true power can be unlocked. It's like seeing your magic plant develop into a massive tree. Sometimes it starts off slowly, but as time goes on, the growth becomes more noticeable. You may enjoy the entire benefits of compounding if you have patience.

7. Reasons to Consider Long-Term Investing

Compounding and long-term investing are like best mates. Your money has more time to go through the compounding cycle the longer you leave it invested. For this reason, the value of being a patient investor is frequently discussed; it's similar to allowing your miracle plant the time it requires to grow into a large, flourishing tree.

8. Start Early, Watch It Grow

The advice to students is very clear: get started early. Over time, your money grows more powerful and gratifying the earlier you lay the seed and allow it to undergo the enchanted compounding process. It's similar to having a money-making tree of your own that gets bigger and stronger with time.

In summary, the power of compounding in long-term investing is similar to a miraculous process of money growth. Students can position themselves for financial success by enabling their investments to grow over time by grasping and accepting this idea early on.

Balancing Risk and Reward in Your Investment Portfolio

1. The investment portfolio is as follows

An individual or entity's holdings of stocks, bonds, mutual funds, real estate, and other financial instruments make up their investment portfolio. It functions similarly to a basket filled with several investments.

2. Risk

The unpredictability or fluctuation of investment returns is referred to as risk. There is risk associated with any investment. Typical forms of risk include interest rate risk, company risk, and market risk, which refers to variations in the market as a whole.

3. Reward

An investor's potential profit or return on investment is referred to as their reward. Investments with a higher potential risk usually yield larger returns than those with a lower potential risk.

4. Balancing Risk and Reward

Finding the ideal mix of risk and return that fits your time horizon, risk tolerance, and financial objectives is essential to successful investment. Each person has a distinct level of risk tolerance; some people can tolerate bigger risks in exchange for a higher potential return, while others would rather take smaller risks for more consistent returns.

5. Diversification

To lower risk, diversification involves dividing investments among several asset classes and industries. Even if one investment does poorly, others might make up for it. It lessens the effect of underperforming assets on the portfolio as a whole.

6. Knowing Your Tolerance for Risk

The ability and willingness of a person to tolerate fluctuations in the market value of their investments is known as their risk tolerance. Before building your portfolio, it's critical to determine your level of risk tolerance to make sure you can stay invested through market ups and downs without acting recklessly.

7. Long-Term Viewpoint

One should consider investments from a long-term standpoint. Although markets have generally demonstrated an upward trend over the long run, they can be volatile in the short term. A crucial component of successful investing is frequent patience.

8. Consistently Tracking and modifying

Financial environments and markets change. Keep a close eye on your portfolio and adjust it as necessary. Rebalancing is changing how assets are allocated in order to preserve the intended risk and return ratio.

Students can create a well-rounded investing strategy that manages the risks involved in investing while also aligning with their financial objectives by understanding and putting these principles into practice. It's critical to remain knowledgeable, ask for help when you need it, and periodically review your investing strategy as your financial circumstances change.

The Impact of Social Media on Financial Decisions

Students' financial decisions are greatly affected by social media, thus it's critical that they understand how social media might affect their behavior. These are important things to remember

1. Information Accessibility

Students have immediate access to a variety of financial information thanks to social media. This covers news, market trends, investment advice, and guidance on personal finances. Although this accessibility is advantageous, students should exercise caution when it comes to the accuracy and reliability of the information they take in.

2. Influence on Investment Choices

- Social media sites frequently feature investor success stories of those who have made substantial financial gains. This may instill a sense of urgency in students and lead them to make snap decisions on investments before fully considering the risks involved.

3. Herding Behavior

Social networking sites may worsen herding behavior, which is the tendency for people to make financial decisions by following the herd. Students might feel pressured to participate in a financial trend or investment that becomes popular on social media without doing the necessary research.

4. Speculation and Market Hype

Hype and speculation in the market can be fueled by social media. Positive or negative opinions about particular companies or investing possibilities may be amplified through discussions, forums, and online groups. Inflated values and heightened market volatility may result from this.

5. Opportunities for Financial Education

Important educational resources can also be found on social media. Tutorials, webinars, and debates that improve financial literacy are available to students. It's essential that students use social media as a learning tool and evaluate the reliability of the content that they encounter.

6. Emotional Impact

Social media can intensify emotional reactions to news about the economy and changes in the market. Information on social media might cause panic selling or fear of missing out (FOMO). Students should endeavor to make logical conclusions based on in-depth analysis and be conscious of the emotional consequences.

7. Internet Fraud & Scams

Financial fraud has the potential to flourish on social media sites. Learners should exercise caution when it comes to internet marketing, and inappropriate investment advice as these might result in financial losses.

8. Privacy Concerns

There are privacy hazards when sharing private financial information on social media. Learners have to exercise caution when sharing anything online and think about the potential consequences of giving out private financial information.

In conclusion, even if social media presents beneficial chances for information exchange and financial education, students need to use caution when using it. Making informed decisions, evaluating information critically, and being conscious of the emotional and behavioral effects that social media may have on financial decisions are all important. Students can better manage the challenges of managing their finances in the digital age by building a solid foundation in financial literacy and consulting reliable sources for advice.

The Rise of FinTech: How Technology is Transforming Finance

For those who are interested in both technology and finance, "The Rise of FinTech: How Technology is Transforming Finance" is a fascinating topic. Let's explore the key ideas

1. Definition of FinTech

Financial technology, or FinTech, is the abbreviation for the use of technology to deliver financial services. It includes a broad range of applications, such as peer-to-peer lending platforms, robo-advisors, blockchain, and mobile banking and payment apps.

2. Digital Banking

Through the introduction of mobile banking apps and digital-only banks, FinTech has completely transformed traditional banking. Through these platforms, consumers may conveniently and easily manage their finances, transfer money, and access a variety of financial services using their smartphones.

3. Payment Innovations

FinTech has revolutionized the way individuals send and receive money. Peer-to-peer payment apps, mobile wallets, and contactless payments have all grown in popularity as quicker and more effective substitutes for cash payments.The greatest example of it is UPI (Unified Payment Interface).

4. Cryptocurrencies and Blockchain

The underlying technology of cryptocurrencies like Bitcoin, blockchain technology, has disrupted established banking structures. It offers a safe and decentralized method of keeping track of transactions. New opportunities for digital transactions, international payments, and decentralized finance (DeFi) applications are provided by cryptocurrencies

5. Robo-Advisors

FinTech uses robo-advisors to provide automated investment advice services. By using algorithms to manage portfolios and offer investment advice, these platforms increase the affordability and accessibility of investing services for a wider group of investors.

6. Peer-to-Peer Lending

Peer-to-peer lending platforms are now possible thanks to FinTech, which eliminates the need for conventional financial middlemen by bringing borrowers and lenders together directly. Lower rates for borrowers and possibly larger returns for lenders can result from this.

7. Insurtech

With the rise of Insurtech, the insurance sector has also witnessed the effects of FinTech. Accurate risk assessment, streamlined insurance procedures, and customized insurance solutions are all made possible by technology.

8. RegTech

RegTech, or regulatory technology, uses technology to make it easier for financial firms to abide by rules. It lowers expenses, streamlined compliance procedures, and improves regulatory reporting efficiency.

9. Financial Inclusion

By offering services to disadvantaged populations, FinTech has significantly contributed to the advancement of financial inclusion. Financial services are now accessible to people in distant or underbanked locations thanks to digital wallets, mobile banking, and microfinance apps.

10. Challenges and Risk

FinTech has many advantages, but it also has disadvantages, including regulatory uncertainty, cybersecurity dangers, and data privacy issues. These difficulties should be recognized by students as they explore the fascinating relationship between technology and finance.

For anyone trying to deal with the changing financial services market in the digital era, as well as for students pursuing professions in finance and technology, understanding the growth of FinTech is important. It presents fascinating chances and difficulties that will continue to influence how the financial sector develops.